JOHN DENNIS

Otherwise

CARCANET

First published in Great Britain in 2015 by
Carcanet Press Limited
Alliance House
Cross Street
Manchester M2 7AQ

www.carcanet.co.uk

A CIP catalogue record for this book is available from the British Library

ISBN 978 1 84777 499 6

The publisher acknowledges financial assistance from Arts Council England

Supported by
ARTS COUNCIL
ENGLAND

Typeset by XL Publishing Services, Exmouth
Printed and bound in England by SRP Ltd, Exeter

For my mother and father,
who named me

Acknowledgements

Acknowledgements are due to the editors of the following, where some of these poems first appeared: *Broadsheet* (NZ), *Contrappasso*, *Critic*, the *Journal of Italian Translation*, *La Libellula*, *New Poetries V* (Carcanet), *New Walk*, *Otago Daily Times*, *PN Review*, *Poetry Proper* and *Turbine*. The completion of this book was made possible by a grant from Creative New Zealand.

Contents

Let us lay down then, lay down
the copious unmarked preserves
of the squirrelling, querulous heart

and return to gratitude — find
the given in our homing,
the word to end all boasting.

Errata

after Eileen Duggan, New Zealand Poems, *1st edn, 1940*

For their death *read* your death;
for I had always *read* I always;
for nothing that *read* nothing can;
for moon *read* mourn;
for limb *read* lamb;
for cuckoo *read* cockerel;
for thundered *read* thundering;
for quiet *read* quake;
for the hills' river *read* the hill's riven;
for Oh *read* Or;
for and if atonement *read* and is atonement;
for there *read* here;
for as *read* so;
for no *read* yes.

These, and other errors, are due to war conditions.

Crookes' Radiometer

Hand-blown; how clear things become
pushed near to breaking point, breath
in the hot glob of dust: the bright form
of the skull. *I opened my mouth*
and drew in my breath: a partial vacuum,
a loosening readiness, raised about a spike,
obsessive pivot round which the vanes hum,
things opting for the flipside, flick!
off the leading edge, the sun's bobbin
threading on – it winds me up no end,
amen, the utter answerability
of the least scintilla leaves me chastened,
my small sphere humming the silicate hymn:
after the dark, the morning and its mercy.

Lone Kauri (reprise)

So take for starters the surge-black fissure,
the waves which register the lunatic sense
it is all well beyond us. Our flooded nature

rages at the dying light, measures
its measures down some lone goat-track,
works up some incorrigible reprise

on grace, etc., a tuning fork
striking itself out of true on the table
of the elements. But blow, burn, break

and be done with it: baptism will
look like this, the flailing, the flensing of waves
and the breath knocked into you, the haul

that finds you first-footing land, brings
the morning. Forgive my making light of
the glass half-empty and you weighing up the dregs;

but I will get up like a love-cast father
awakening to children's voices, the night-
time true underfoot, who hears their laughter

and finds, at the unclosed door, the seam of light.

Northwards

In the way I stall
under the oncoming headlight
of each ancient train,

this acupuncture of light,
the weightless years that advance,
recede, the dot-to-dot surveillance

of our listless twitching, driving.
Off the surface of Waihola
they cover us.

There is relief only in waiting
for the rind to roll under us,
a brief valve in our atmospheres.

Who moves? Do we rear earthily
into the black Taieri hills, or does Orion,
his blue diamonds worn long over cool indigo,

slip into the wings?

The Call

for Fyfe Blair

The rain passes. Away on the edge of town,
the geese lift, gaining difficultly
in the thin morning, a congregation welling up
out of muddied fields, and rising into
the burnishing west, breasting the hill-shot air.

I watch them go, a dream of wing-beat and assent
beyond say-so, beyond call, and I long
for the swoop and grab by the scruff of the neck, the unquestioning,
unlooked-for lift out of this menagerie,
this forsaken plot, the proving ground of love.

To Keep Warm Inside

Under the bitter yoke
of these red untempered mornings,

steer the car like a life-raft
down Cumberland to this

crystal palace, this sometime church.
Tiles, and the wall of light

steaming across the variegated
blues of February.

The liquid aisles, lightly ushering,
rope the depth beneath,

declining order: fast,
medium, slow; aquajoggers

descend and return
shallow from deep. Receive

the goggled epiphany: limbs
flaying out the imagined ellipse, torsos

strapped just buoyant below the surface,
striving for peace or perfection;

in Dunedin – steamed open like a cockle
this morning in mid-July.

The Garden

for Paul and Maddie

You step from the house into the garden;
the light gathers in your wake
and lets loose, falling across the kitchen
threshold. In the summer dusk,

the light gathers in. You wake
as you home across London's
threshold in the summer dusk,
into the sanctuary, a promise held open

for you – home across London
to sit down at the table together. Now you walk
into the sanctuary: a promise held open,
the joining of hands – love speaks

and sits down at the table. Together now you walk
the walls of a small garden; nothing to darken
the joining of hands. Love speaks:
some things bear repeating, and those things lighten

the walls of a small garden, nothing to darken
you sitting to write, dream, seek
those things that bear repeating. And something lightens
as you gather folk and make them welcome – there is joy to mark

you setting dreams to rights. Seek,
and let loose. Calling across the kitchen
you gather folk and make welcome. Here, then, is joy to mark
you. Step from the house into the garden.

Nocturne

Drawn in the shallow breath of the night,
I wait for you to come back home,
willing the shadows to find your form;

but how can they carry your bright step,
the house of light that is your face?
My lighthouse, my love, the rocks are night all around.

Standing on the porch, I drive these backroads –
some hurt unwinding, some dry-mouthed valley,
and the sounds – drab, surd syllables:

the cough of a sheep;
the hills, their sodden bales as they slump;
small branches fret the roofing iron.

Turn, heart, turn – go back home;
leave this road unwound.

Clarities

Scotland was a westerly and a had-it Aga,
miles away from the nearest and with anger
milling. It was a full table, our families
all arms, the kids scrapping and feral

after the main was over and the pudding still
to come; we fell to talking opacities,
all quip and allusion lightly round the tipping
point, heart's overflow, his mouth pumped

by the flywheel of a sick, decentred love:
boy-grown-man still wants his father's yes,
that usual story which underlies too much
then cuts across a marriage like a spring-

tooth harrow used drunk. Now, Kincaple!
think of that small farmhouse to your east,
the pre-teen's rile, her mother's siloed grist;
call the unseen guest to the potluck table.

Sleepers

Friends decide to separate. After,
we enter the clearing, retrace our steps. A fine
rain settles, and everything is un-
accountably beautiful, unaccountable,
being not promised. Promise – it hung
in the air over the improvised picnic table,
between the opened faces; we nearly sang.
Depressions in the grass, the shape of laughter.
All that time the lines lay, unconverging,
fiercely gauged off each other, overgrown in the dirt –
now ripped out like spade-struck fencing wire,
turf turned and agape the length of the clearing.
We look down. *Gutted for you, mate.*
And there, unrotted, their pitch glinting, the sleepers.

Promissory

Love, I never looked to find us here:
the night below, spreading like a slick,
we hurtle the heart's acres, wanting the clear
line lifting from the cutting. The track,
even so, shines as if bio–
luminescent, promissory and mutual,
so that we come through things, so
that the sleepers sheet into a blurred still,
and the siding waste and hedging, the miry verge,
are made to fall behind. What was purposed
when by grace we vowed to enter marriage
was quite beyond us: we shone undiverted
into the way of things, not alone
ever again, profoundly moved towards home.

Tawa

Thinly yellow, and fibrous in the heat,
fennel is legion, rank beside the lines,
which shimmer, robing the air in a ferrous stink.
Flowchart rampant! The stalk, and then the branchings,
mnemonic of throughput and outcome, of progress
and its needling filiform leaf, the scent so hard
to shake. Do not consider the flowers, the seed
falling across the sleepers. There, sudden
between the tracks, a penetrative, metro-
nomic knocking from a torso-like box,
locked and knocking in the valley of your childhood.
O dark kernel, o burr of ambition,
remember the boy in his switch-flicking trance
in love not with the light, but with the switching.

Pitched

The night's lateness comes down early
and you're relegated to the loo. Unlooked for,
and all natural enough. But how surely

we lose our grip: the kids' door
across the hall blanks like a fart,
surgent, unsignifying to the floor:

fear fear, shake shake! The intimate dark
pitches and sheets as the motions go through
(let the reader understand: our opaque art).

So much – there there – is what passes for you:
the frame the (hinge) dear (hinge) values the shape
of things to come? We know not what we do:

we are so otherwise, and elsewhere lies our hope.

Psalm

You ok, sweetheart? What's this, what's this?
You lost someone, sweetheart? Your mum?
Where's your mum, darling? You don't think she'll miss

you out here, in your ballet clothes? You come
with me, we'll find your mum, it will
be ok, it will be. Is this your home?

No? Maybe we should wait until
she comes to find you. You know, try with
me to remember, what did she tell

you before you dropped in the undergrowth,
before I came up off the road,
heard the small bird, fluttering in your mouth?

It's normal – hell, I'd be concerned –
but, you know, the thing is this:
you're lost, right, but in the end

strangely love has appeared to us,
and looking back, we're in good hands.
But I know right now you can't see this.

So I reckon we'll just sit tight. That's a plan.

Source to Sea

for Rebekah and Mark

What is this turning mystery,
this juncture, this opening in the land?
Love traces the river from source to sea,
the distance covered in the joining of your hands.

This juncture, this opening in the land
a train draws itself through, inexorably,
the distance covered. In the joining of your hands
the track leaps ahead to fresh inland seas –

a train draws itself through. Inexorably,
the walled city reveals its gardens; now found,
the track leaps ahead to fresh inland seas,
lanes where coupling bicycles unwind.

The walled city reveals its gardens now. Found
wandering together, visiting love's untidy
lanes where coupling bicycles unwind,
you will camp in each other's mercy.

Wandering together, visiting love's untidy
red telephone boxes, you understand
you will camp in each other's mercy.
All this movement: lips meet; you find

red telephone boxes; you understand
love traces the river. From source to sea,
all this – movement – lips meet – you find
what is this turning mystery.

Watermarks

for Claire Beynon

Engines ahead of us and we're drawn,
another journey beginning in darkness;

we go through the cutting,
faces half-selving on the double glazing –

now fading into the slate dawn.
The train's refrain picks up –

particular, particular, particularly –
as everything waxes,

bruised light letting down
on wet hollows, fields harrowed, wheat on the turn.

Eyes follow the soft verge,
a certain line of questioning falling over

hedges, grounded rooks,
sheds, suggestions of thresholds;

and always engines ahead,
the thudding haul as we hug the embankment.

Black sycamores, and the pale green arrangements
of caravans give out,

the firth blurring into view –
a charcoal feathering of sight,

furthering over the immaculate surface:
all gradation, all meniscus,

fine grit and water,
sea holding weed holding stone holding

our brief gaze wavering along the lines,
and the morning lifts into the opaque horizon:

light's hesitations at the pointedness of everything.
People on the beach pause and stare again –

a train passing above water,
a fine hand drawn across paper,

sky heavy above with water,
and herring gulls cry in the wheels.

Soaked

The corbelled, shuttered town,
and the heart all cobble and kerb,
this day won't open here,
no scope and reach under
the elegiac forms,
the epaulette-laden trees,
and Mary's crutched thorn.
But cut out of the town
round by Magus Muir
and climb through Strathkinness,
drop the high road down,
wing-off the gabled make-dos,
the northing, estuarine views
and sit back in the saddle,
the westerly just abreast
so that the wind-rush hushes
and all that is left is the fluid
thrum on the metal: and the larks
loosen their wee spigots
over the scoured fields
so that the air runs, fills
the gutters of the day and you.

Blackbird

after the Irish, ninth century

This wee bird
whistling from
a gorse-gold
       beak – blackbird! –

lets fly over
the inlet
from a heap
       of yellow.

Catechesis, St Andrews

Come by me now; do you recall
the cliffs of Castle Beach, and how
the rock laid bare its laden belts

of life let down? The pronounced black seam
in the sedimentary crumble, proof against progress
or success — yours, or any other

in the graduated powers of our step-
gabled, end-stopped city (*your name
here, high and distorting on the over-*

taut awning!) Come by and stand,
empty at last in your mastery,
at the edge of what you'd presumed was there

for the taking, and taking so much for granted;
you are not your own, any more than the fulmars
that ride this airy conjunction, not knowing

they do what they do and so in their way
are better servants than you, who was bought with a price
and, knowing this, still put on airs.

So here, you might turn away from the drop,
murmuring with relief, *it's all relative, it's all good,
you should just try harder, be true, be free,*

and so forget the bells at your back:
not *all good*, but well: is, and shall be.
Come by, sweet-heart: East Neuk, North Sea,

Bell Rock, the Eden estuary;
how the westerly ramps up and over-shoots
your situation entirely,

unrelentingly plays on the levelled, in-shore
face of things before us. What is it
required of you? Repeat after me.

Triptych

in memory of Seamus Heaney

I
Grace Note
17 June 2013

The walls stepping back apace;
the late, high, western sun
declining any impulse to grace

ourselves, be otherwise than
our falling shadows, our homing faces
reveal we are. And then:

a drink? A whiskey? The capacious
front room, quiet talk, the telly
cutting to Obama in Belfast,

while the critic in me
is weaned. Dublin Bay
takes up the slack – *the*

incarnation sets us free for play –
(sure, no truer word spoken);
I'm suitably censered, you might say.

Poet, bless me three times, even!

II
Postcard
James Nairn, Wellington Harbour, *1894*

Dear S, meant to send this some time back.
Thought you'd recognise the scene well enough:
in the foreground, a woman walks with a stick,
set in her own shadow as in her love,
the face a heavy dab of grief, a desire
to be elsewhere. Lately the waters rise,
and in brightness the sheds and the wharf lower
as the man, darkling, is held. What remains
is that a gulf exists; and the true poem,
our boat beyond all making, floats adjacent,
its shocking mast crossing the horizon
so that we might see, in this moment,
how truly the water gives us back the light.
Hope all well; not sure if you'll get this all right.

III
Touch and Go

The day remembers itself to a sky-blown dusk,
light still coming off the small cloths which ride
the sagging line. Inside, the family play hide and seek,

all our early numbers mounting so confident
to the coming ready or not, while everybody scatters,
loses themselves so easily. And with this: blackbird,

his brief wise-o exile song, a smatter
of grace notes struck out at the gable-end.
So: we're held, heart-pegged, hung in the matter

of things counted out, and hid, and found –
appeasing knowledge of song, and of our folly.
Wait here over-long for what doesn't come again,

translates away, across, and up the gully.

Fallen Oak

after Giovanni Pascoli

Now, the oak falls into its shadow,
dead – no more tussling with the wind.
Look, people say, how great!

Tangled in the crown, the tiny nests
of spring dangle and tilt; of course,
folk say, how true, how good!

Everyone talks it up, then takes a cut –
come nightfall, each makes off with a hefty stack.
In the airy clearance, high cries… the blackbird

is looking for her nest; she will not find it.

To a Cousin

Dear K, please don't mind my writing like this –
allow me, undergrowth to your staggered
reach, some momentary airiness
over the leaves. Turn the page, and
here's much you'd recognise: the quiet avarice
of suburbia, the western hills a long rummage
in the handbag; sudden anger at the noise
of unseen children; the risen dust on the ridge;
and in the dark embankment gully hydrangeas,
the leaves catching a fall of light, their undersides
the careful work of loving hands, sure as
the morning, though the sky is pale and hides
its unstinting address. Who witnesses
finds, among great trees, assurances.

Reed

Isaiah 42:3

To turn here, rain brightening the trail
ahead, and stand, thoughts shaking and lame –
my doubtful fingers read the bole-cast braille
where some king of fools cut his name;
slow fire: see how the sap's running mirth
must stigmatise us – we bleed to grow.
Tall – a scaffold lifting from the earth,
sky-thrasher, a swelling of shadow –
now, torn, tongues let loose, the shattered crown
pours out its rushing supplication;
fleshy grasses, outstripping the ground,
run blindly from the flaming, from
the wind that scores its song in us and
this tree – *our Father!* – clapping its hands.

Crossing

for my sons

What was it (o, mortal), that hurt I was led
back through, as they lifted the mattress?

The way back plain enough, beloved: fear
of losing what I desired most; disdain

of others; the guilt of thoughtlessness that
registers, normally, only in

momentary lameness, in the fumbled cup;
and shame – enough of that, sitting down to

breakfast. Then, yes, the lies gleaned in the verge
of others' well-cut minds, quick in the mouth and

mingling with the unreal names to keep you
reeling. And all what else – love forbids these here –

all that. Beloved, there were other things:
school's long line-up; me, at the heady top

in mute one-upmanship, pitying Kelvin –
fat antithesis who cried in his

self-knowledge, covered my desk in vomit
that afternoon bright with dust. I did not

laugh: desperate watching that lumbering
non-starter, I knew I would sit also,

pulling grass, waiting to be picked, self-
circumscribed also-ran, the body

(excellent fidelity!) disappointing
in the execution. Unreal the names

that are not lifted from us. And then (my
little children!) I cannot say what else:

these things were before, are beyond telling,
names, marks, laid down in a hard drive against

the grain – the from whom and through whom and
to whom are all things – and what lifts,

splintering, is need, a mouth to hurt her breast;
also pain, the twisted foot in the chambered heart.

All this I laid me down; from all was I
let down through the lifting roofing iron

into love's bare answer, the room crowding
with familiars' background noise, marks, names,

making sure of themselves – heartfelt appeal:
justice be done and seen to be done – my

Lord. Which is easier to say? Well,
the sign is what the maker does. And did.

Beloved, I was undone truly. And all
that now lifted from me, below, so dry

on the dry watershed, the mounding cairn
well below the high and swinging crossing.

The Manner of Your Leaving

So much is known, and is beyond us still:
leave we must, beloved, until

we are gone from here, and the tree hangs
its empty nests for longer than it takes

to fill them, the dusk empty of birdsong
and the city committed to the ground of its unforgetting.

We cannot say how, so that some
are gone already, beloved, even one

I played with as a boy, a man I loved
in my unthinking way; I admired

his skill, overlooked too much his gentleness.
And these memories (this poem, reader!) also

must take their leave, be left by the minds
that cling to them unrelieved; but exactly how,

in what sheet-winding procedure,
body and spirit come unstuck

is too much for simple time to reveal,
except in the unsticking, the winding. Dust

is a dead metaphor; and the theme repeats
its variations, of which this is one: what suspense

remains is the manner of your leaving – is that it?
That is not it. And we don't have a choice

in the matter! When all is said and done,
stand weeping outside the tomb,

beside the rolling stone, see
the God-forsaken winding sheets,

in the manner of your leaving.

The House was Full

Lights off and the last to leave, we paused
in the porch to pray – no bees, Jim Baxter,
but the night air was humming. Overhead,

the streetlights' big reach and put-down of
the night, a *no limits* and *got it covered* – such
chipper polity (in a slightly jaundiced light)!

But here's the thing: the house was full behind me,
fullness personal and knowing, hands
raised in the mothering grammar and urging us

on across the threshold and up the slope.
Call it what you will – communion of saints,
a cloud of witnesses – they dance as lights

dance in the periphery of vision.

A Brief History of the Sign

Christ Jesus is ane A per C,
And peirlesse Prince of all mercy.
                    Gude and Godlie Ballates

O we amplify, admire you,
most elaborate abbreviation,

here & here we dither
in your twisting compact,

roundabout shortcut, my bicycle
of punctuation, we trace

your winding path over &
over, hands bent & doubling

to receive or pass you by,
a labyrinthine prayer,

a club-footed coupling.
Wee quirk of a curled mark!

Mute word holding
such things together –

things visible & invisible,
to love & to hold,

on heaven & on earth –
O magnify:

              &

Madonna and child!

43

House Concert in the Shadowlands

for Will and Alison

All around, his guitar, like a windfall pear,
dark-centred and the sweetness giving over,
dark as the bourbon which rises in the jar
the colour of *pollo en mole poblano*,
dark loamy as the eyes of Eden
your astonishing daughter, friends.
And won't this come again, won't
we again pause and lift our heads
to the note rising, and us with it?
O Mary Ursula Bethell, you –
gardening – made poetry on your knees!
How truly found are the lilies
you held out for, how sharp-scented,
how blooming good are they?

The Immanent Frame

She twists in her seat to face
the sudden reach of glass
through which all is quick,
which quivers itself.

Her forehead and high eyebrows
are stripped high, the long
growth of hair scaled
back into something manageable,

so that the eyes are lit
largely outwith the face,
her cheekbones lifting under
the skin in an effort of delicacy.

Absorbed, we believe, except
that her attention is not an arm-span, is digital:
fingers rubber-scraping
condensation into paths,

wee causeways, perhaps, through
the sea of peopled air?
But no, the fine
prints make a trail

of breathlessness, the fingered erasure
of all this, our briefly
lightening water, before
it all lightly steams

back into bloom. So,
she signs off, staring
and scraping on panes shuddering
with the diesel push of it all,

while all the while is carried
through, unsensing each
extra mile which goes
itself.

After Geering

And we're like
oh my *god* like

it's so true like,
he was saying:

Life has become a venture?
in which each of us is now responsible?
for creating our own personal meaning system?

You know like *god*, like
I just find it so relatable; it's like

her thready rondure and the stitched

name of Levi Strauss, below the patch
  seeking.

Like *god* like, feel me up Scotty! The sign is like
what the maker – you know:

Hell-oh! Like,
my God why have you like,

forsaken me why are you
so far from like,

saving me? Like,
he grew up before the Lord like

a young plant, and like
a root out of dry ground;

he had no form or majesty that we should look at him,
nothing in his appearance that we should desire him.

47

He was despised and rejected by others; a man
of suffering and acquainted with infirmity; and like

one from whom others hide their faces
he was despised, and we held him of no account.

And he was poured out like
water.

On Climate Change

As you fill your car again
do not forget who carried Balaam:
that it was she who, naturally,
saw the whetted danger ahead
standing in the wilful path
of the sold-out say-so. And remember
that she did not balk, but went to pasture.
Instinct with self-possession,
he beat her surely back into
his way of things. This proved –
moving forward – a tighter squeeze,
stones like waves of the crowding sea;
Balaam's gut, equivocal,
quivered in the scrape with the vineyard wall.
But he asserted his wiggle*raum*
and manned up with a beating,
so even this near-thing was
theorised well enough. Then?
Then a narrow place, where
there was no way to turn either
to the right or to the left.
And naturally she saw, and lay
her down faithful, and let down
her brute master with unassuming
prescience. So the excellent visionary,
straddling the quiet back, got
stuck in; the dust rose and infused
the air around, the blood in his mouth,
blood of her flanks. Now, as you
squat again over a patch of this earth,
glancing down to see your water
puddles cleanly – not splashing
your un-hairy legs – listen
again to her God-given rebuke;
see what it is waits, sword drawn.

Ecce

for Marco

I

Some kind of good meal,
I recall, our insult to injury there,
in the absolute city, Calcutta: callus

of endless pavement, my unrequited.
After, we trot along, un-
backpacked; and in the midst, the river,

its sure progress: come cross, come die.

II

He lies in our path, matted instance
of a general sliding rule, and the opened
body is eloquent: the clavicles,

their drained cups mouth the Psalmist's
drouth: *I am a worm, and not human;*
scorned by others, and despised by the people.

All who see me mock at me; they make
their mouths at me, they shake their heads.
Ecce the pelvis, mounding under.

Ecce. O my goodness; my god.

III

O we pass by, yes, and there is an
end of it, wayward in the way we mouth
ruefulness, say, or appropriate concern,

so that, having passed, we labour with
the air, with balance – any progress this way
is hard-fought, self-won, wrath

as a mounding under: *incurvatus in se*.
And isn't this where we find ourselves,
some few steps past and the impulse to stray,

not turn to the body who addresses
us with wasted abnegation?
Here, beloved (o come alongside us!)

in two minds, perhaps, now turn.

IV

He is, I guess, my age; wasted
and guttingly light; this much I carry
still: the sit bones set in distressed

relief under his shorts, the bleary
taxi driver and his concern
over upholstery as he ferries

us to Kalighat. What do we earn
by such? The doorman's bald rebuke
at the door – 'you need to phone

to let us know you're coming'; the lock
tumbles, and in we go, arms full
of life at the end of the tether, and back

out to the car, raging and pitiful.

V

Ecco fatto. And nothing earned.
Things are, in fact, otherwise,
so that brought close to the agony

of the final taxi ride, we find
those small tally sticks amount
to so much kindling. We warm ourselves

and talk quietly, breakfasting on the beach
at the crossing, and dare not ask who it is
tends the fire, who will lift us, arm

under shoulder, under hip – *nirmal hriday.*

Seeing it Through

Ferdinand Hodler, The Sick Valentine Godé-Darel, *1914*

After all, your eyes, hand,
will traverse the contours nearly,

things unfinished turning together
not unlike landscape, but artless,

aware of what rises in the bone –
knowing we are prone to it, and must see

it through. And isn't that just so?
God help us, you make your bed

and lie in it. Honestly. And time was
when you saw it plain. But look,

here's the thing, the contours of your passing:
folds and fells of bedclothes mounding

to a horizon of opaque deposits, and these
laid over an unrelieved presence, your head,

blankly enhaloed, and the lips red.
Truly, beloved, we are not perspicuous

to ourselves; we are drawn still by death's
gas-mask bouquet setting at the end

of what we've made of it, a stopper, a knocker,
a mouth that denies the art that becomes us –

through which we might see (lift mine eyes)
that the world's high clock is hanged

by a cross. And how. Hold the sheet
up to the light: see your face coming through.

There's One Straight Out of the Box

we are monads, haunted by communion
— George Steiner

I

Stalled. I have been here before – the door
jars, jacks brittle against the frame,
the latch tacky with shed life; and then, *before*

was indistinct, of no moment, the same
squared-off address of flashings and vitreous bowl,
an unfocused grey of tiles and melamine

strict about the flush, cyclopic control
and confessional; so much slips my mind.
I dangle myself absently over the flow,

hear the shuffle and held breath behind
the partition, and try to feel elsewhere.
There, cramped in the grouting, the small hand

of diminished hope: *I was here.*

II

Up above my head there's music in the air,
emoting and riffs ecstatic, a levity
of unsensing. You may not inquire

of this; flush-mounted in the cavity,
it gasses sweetly as a smoked hive,
while the pressure drops and all amity

is let go for the stacked groove,
glottal coagulate, a *geist*-heist
tendering: desire becomes us. Wave

at the sensor. So much passes for protest,
begs the question: wherefore fullness, and thanks –
where is the love? We long to rest,

loosely shackled in our downed pants.

III

It's reassuring to suppose that beyond
this is another much the same,
that what we have and give in common

is a faced and floating panelling – axiom
of our lately closed circuit, it will trump
neighbourliness, the open, cupped palm,

dam us in a right to do: we jump
at the latch fumble, *I'm in here!*
i.e. *piss off!* Ach, we do not make up

the world, truly – your suspended enclosure
is not the henceforth longed for!
Sit still: feet at the door, the knock, and you're

caught in the one-two altogether!

IV

Once open, the door is beside the point, the point
being – say it! – reconciliation,
yes, now there's one straight out of the box,

a notion worth a line or two on
grouting, say, or the Kelburn church wall –
God does not live in boxes – amen

to that brother, and as for us, all
our constructs might flat-pack it off, we lose
our thrones as the sky grows tall, forsake the cubicle

for an opened upper room. And there's grace:
not to be going out or coming in
but set in the threshold, your solar plexus rise

and fall in step with all who are undone.

This Just One Thing

Late, you don't know the half,
and at the end of the day I'm at it,
the tethered end: this self–

reflexive, monographical effort.
'[N]o acceptable religious position that is not a reinforce-
ment of human responsibility' (Leavis on Eliot);

well, the reality is; and of course
I'm banging on with the responsibility
of it all, turn the page, hit the space

key again, hit control, and glory
be but I cannot sing myself clean,
but hit return, control, hit the space key.

And the cleaner comes. In unconcern,
in measure, she bags the dust,
elects, in the darkened hall, the un–

resourceful person. O lift
at the discourse as you sing: sing
about every knee bowed, and death –

so may I do this just one thing –
about tongues, his rising, and the Lord.
And she has the poem, cleaning and singing,

as through her dances the crowning word.

The Extra Mile

for my mother and father

At first I turned out other than
I should have been, both my feet
ponga fronds uptight and uncurling,
wee question marks at the end

of the good *let there be*,
distempered parts questioned in turn,
yes, by compassion, sharply,
and turning out right enough

to be going on with, my unloosed ends.
Love marked me; love shaped me;
and this mothering grammar holds
good still. At my birth,

Was Gott tut, das ist wohlgetan,
my father sang with the Bach chorale,
and what is done has entered me,
left me longing for the extra mile.